ARNOLD WESKER

ARNOLD
WESKER

by

GLENDA LEEMING

Edited by Ian Scott-Kilvert

PUBLISHED FOR
THE BRITISH COUNCIL
BY LONGMAN GROUP LTD

LONGMAN GROUP LTD
Longman House, Burnt Mill, Harlow, Essex

*Associated companies, branches and
representatives throughout the world*

First published 1972
© Glenda Leeming, 1972

*Printed in Great Britain by
F. Mildner & Sons, London, EC1R 5EJ*

SBN 0 582 01225 2

ARNOLD WESKER

I

MORE than any of his contemporaries among the new dramatists, Arnold Wesker tempts critics and audiences to discuss the subject matter of his plays as if it were real life, ignoring its form, its presentation, its purposeful internal relationships. Once this temptation is overcome, however, the total shape of each play takes on additional dimensions of irony, of reservation and qualification, of unexpected poetic vision, so that the direct and immediate appeal of the usually colourful, vigorous characters and incidents falls into place as only a part of what the dramatist has to offer.

In fact much of the material in the plays *has* an obvious origin in real life—that is, in Wesker's own life. The son of a Russian-Jewish tailor, he was born in 1932 in the East End of London. Many of the situations in the first five plays were, he has said, drawn directly from his own experience—though sometimes with deliberate alterations. His mother was a communist, for example, like Sarah in *Chicken Soup with Barley*, and his sister and brother-in-law tried to escape the pressures of city life by moving out to a cottage in Norfolk, like the central characters of *I'm Talking about Jerusalem*. Since he began writing adolescent poetry in imitation of this admired brother-in-law, Wesker had intended to be a writer, and in 1950 he recorded the progress of his initial National Service training in the Royal Air Force in a series of letters he then reworked into a novel—material he later used in *Chips with Everything*. However, after his National Service he did what is arguably the opposite of starving in the poet's traditional garret and became a professional pastry-cook. Although he had felt the attraction of amateur acting for many years, he used the

money saved during two years of this work in Paris to enter
the London School of Film Technique, and it was the twin
stimuli of *The Observer* 1957 play competition—for which
his entry *The Kitchen* was disqualified as too short—and the
impact of Osborne's epoch-making *Look Back in Anger* in
1956 that propelled him definitely away from the film
industry and into the theatre.

The generation that created the mid- and late-fifties
revival in British drama had in common a subjection to the
pressures of a world war in early youth, and subsequently
a disillusionment with a brave new world that settled into
a more affluent version of the old; and though none of the
individual dramatists originally knew each other or sub-
scribed to any common literary 'movement', their work
underwent such cross-influences as that of *Look Back in
Anger* on Wesker, who recalls that he 'just recognized that
things could be done in the theatre, and immediately went
home and wrote *Chicken Soup*', first performed in 1958. He
at once began planning *Roots* and in the same year he
married. His wife had been a waitress in a Norfolk hotel
just like Beatie, the heroine of *Roots*, but—another example
of experience being reshaped into art—Wesker elliptically
points out that Ronnie, his equivalent in the play, becomes
an entirely different person by virtue of his evasiveness.
'I married my wife: Ronnie in *Roots* does not.'

In 1961 several people including the world-famous
philosopher Bertrand Russell and a young English playwright Arnold Wesker were jailed for peacefully demon-
strating against nuclear weapons. The recognition Wesker
won in the fifties—an Arts Council award in 1958, the
Evening Standard Most Promising Playwright Award in
1959—focused attention on his political activities, and the
anti-nuclear Committee of One Hundred's aim of arousing
public opinion naturally benefited from his involvement.
Also during 1961 he became Director of the Centre Forty-
two movement which aimed to break down the barriers of
class-consciousness, commercialism and intellectual snob-

bery that it believed were keeping ordinary people from an awareness of the arts. After mounting six regional festivals that were artistic but not financial successes, Centre Forty-two limped on throughout the sixties, mainly trying to establish one real centre in the Roundhouse in London, an impressive disused Victorian engine shed, its lease acquired at further great expense. An appeal failed to raise the vast sum necessary for the full conversion of this huge circular building, and when Centre Fortytwo was officially dis-solved in 1970 the Roundhouse and Wesker parted com-pany: the Roundhouse in the course of earning its keep had been hired out to various performing groups and had won a valuable place among the crop of unconventional theatrical arenas which at this period began to challenge London's traditional theatres; concurrently Wesker's own ideas on popular arts centres had evolved towards a concept of something more local, more grass-roots, less ready-made.

Although *Chips with Everything* had all the vigour and colour of the earlier plays, and in 1962 gave Wesker his first and only full scale, long-running West End success, his work during the sixties became less documentary and immediate in impact, with a corresponding decline in popularity but, in compensation, a more evident claim on thoughtful critical response. At the same time he had ex-perienced a revulsion against the commercial processes of play production, even that of the highly sympathetic English Stage Company at the Royal Court Theatre, where so many of the new English dramatists, including Wesker, were first sponsored. In this respect the changing theatrical climate of the sixties is reflected, in the sense that fringe or 'alternative' theatres (like the Roundhouse) staging more and more unconventional performances, came into in-creasing competition with the established playhouses. John Arden, for instance, at a similar point in his playwriting career, also rejected the West End, directing his own play *The Hero Rises Up* at the Roundhouse in 1968 to a mixed critical reception, and concurrently experimenting with techniques of caricature and comic-strip style presentation. Wesker, on the other hand, directing his own play *The Friends* at the Roundhouse in 1970 without great critical success, was breaking new ground not in techniques of presentation, but in his increasingly introspective subject-matter.

Unusually enough, Wesker believes that a writer's life and his work *should* be regarded as a whole: this he states in a collection of lectures and articles, *Fears of Fragmentation* (1970), the title of which, like the belief, suggests a key theme that is consistently developed through the plays. This is E. M. Forster's theme of 'only connect'; the urgent demand that everyone should learn to understand the inter-actions and cross-influences in their lives, how things fit together. The disease of fragmentation cripples the charac-ters in the plays by hiding from them how other facets of society, other unrecognized aspects of life, are affecting them: fragmentation screens from them the connexions which explain why they so often suffer and are helpless. Thus Centre Fortytwo was founded to break down the compartmentalizing (or fragmentation) that classified art as unsuitable for ordinary people; and Wesker later revised his ideas towards an even closer integration of a community and its cultural activity. From saying that he would like people to know him not only by his writing but by his life, he goes on to hope that, ideally, people will know also the writing of his contemporaries; and also their music and painting; and also their social context; and also their society's philosophy and development; so that a new under-standing of unified human activity will allow action to spring from knowledge rather than violent impulse. The plays comment on this ideal of imaginative comprehension, and Wesker's refusal to dissociate his work from his life is a reminder that no detail can be dismissed as slick writing or theatrical flourish: the plays have the whole weight of their writer's character behind them.

II

The shorter version of *The Kitchen* (first performed in 1959) was expanded—mainly by more detailed drawing of the characters and their interrelationships—into its rather longer final form in 1961. In the same year the film version was released, with its highly realistic picture of a steamy, sweaty, noisy hotel basement, but this realism was quite alien to the expressionistic use of the set in the stage play. For the almost plot-less action is not so much about what a number of men do in a kitchen as what the kitchen does to them. The dehumanizing effect of turning out two thousand indifferent meals a day under terrific pressure is made to typify the dehumanizing effect of *all* mass production, and the kitchen itself with its incessantly hissing ovens and looming equipment functions as a concrete symbol, as well as a specific example, of the system. Within this monster, the cooking of meals is mimed by the actors, not only for practical reasons but also to counterpoise the engrossingly convincing routine, and to underline this symbolism, this typicality behind the flow of realistic action. Already Wesker's driving interest in how man and environment shape each other was determining the outward form of his work.

The formal shape of *The Kitchen* is in fact surprisingly controlled: the apparently casual, haphazard texture of the action disguises its overall shape and its internal pattern. The first important point is that one complete, typical day is traced in *The Kitchen*, and this very completeness and typicality is a means of suggesting the monotonous imprisonment of its characters' working life. This day is infinitely repeatable, and such a cyclical form, repressive in its implications, is used by Wesker to substantiate his explicit theme of the dehumanizing pressures of work. The play shows the uneventful interaction of the cooks and porters, from the hardened older men Alfredo and Max to the young, likeable Hans and Dimitri; but as the play opens

the advent of a new cook, Kevin, makes his exploration of
a new job correspond to the audience's exploration of the
kitchen world. Then the two services of lunch and dinner—
when activity becomes frenetic and tempers are exacer-
bated—provide two natural climaxes separated by the cooks'
off-duty break, spent by many of them still in the dominating setting of the kitchen. The stormy love affair of Monica,
a married waitress with the young, excitable German boy
Peter is sketched quickly at intervals during the play, and it
is Peter's frenzy at a seemingly final rejection by Monica
that provides the dramatic climax when the young cook
flies at the gas-pipes with an axe and puts the ovens, and
thus the kitchen, out of action. The play's cyclical shape,
then, is significant, and the tense or relaxed action and
dialogue carefully matched to the normal rhythms of kitchen
routine.

Although the high pressure of turning out meals during
the service frays tempers and underlines the uncooperative
attitude of each character towards the others, this theme of
compartmentalization, of failed communication, is developed more explicitly during the leisure period, particularly by Paul, the articulate Jewish pastry-cook. He has
already noticed inconsistencies in his own behaviour, but
what he finds overwhelmingly frightening are patches of
blank non-sympathy in a usually friendly neighbour, the
'horror' that 'there's a wall, a big wall between me and
millions of people like him'. Yet in the actual environmental
factors that condition their unimaginative narrowness, he
also finds one line of hope to appear in the play: the hope
that more humane conditions may breed more humane
people, on the evidence that, at that very moment, the often
aggressive cooks are finding the peace to understand each
other.

For Peter's violence at the conclusion is a false hope: his
gesture is purely destructive and he is what a later play calls
'a rebel not a revolutionary'. Previously Paul had asked
what could replace the monstrous kitchens, factories and

offices, as people would go on demanding food, wireless sets and even administration by paper-work, and this is the question on which the play ends: what must be taken into account, what must be added to the inadequate system to make it satisfying? It is characteristic of Wesker to conclude with such a question, asked here by the kitchen's owner, Marengo. Why is the saboteur not grateful when he is given food and money: 'What is there more? What is there more? What is there more?'

III

If *The Kitchen* was a prologue to Wesker's playwriting career, the trilogy formed by his next three plays established his reputation, particularly in its sustained ability to approach complex problems from differing angles. The first of these three plays, *Chicken Soup with Barley* (1958), totally unlike *The Kitchen*, deals with the life of the Kahn family over a period of years. In 1936 the energetic Sarah and the rather weaker Harry are both involved in the historic anti-Fascist demonstration in Cable Street, and they and their children Ada and Ronnie are at the centre of a neighbourly, united crowd of active friends. In contrast the last scene shows the older, weary but indomitable Sarah as the last to cling to her communism and to a faith in social progress; every other member of the original community has become disillusioned in a depressingly negative, often selfish way, and Sarah is fighting to rekindle some saving spark of idealism in her son.

This important scene was actually written first, and the form of the play between opening and closing situations represents a series of downward steps as youthful optimism declines into desperation, each stage marked by the alienation of a friend. Paradoxically Sarah's very enthusiasm is responsible for the disaffection of those closest to her: her ideals are so uncompromising that Ada despairs not only of reorganizing society, but of even coping with people whom she regards as appallingly unworthy of her mother's boundless sympathy. Harry, on the other hand, cannot himself live up to Sarah's standards, and his rather lazy evasiveness only increases with her attacks upon it, until a half-wished-for physical paralysis leaves him helpless—justified in his inertia. Ronnie, too, has shared Sarah's vision so absolutely that the shock of disillusionment—in his case following the repressed Hungarian Revolution of 1956; and, simultaneously, with human brotherhood because of the brutal stupidity of his fellow-workers—pushes him to the opposite extreme of apathetic cynicism.

Although the play is faithfully realistic in its dialogue—Sarah's final impassioned speech is still convincingly characteristic of her, neither formalized nor over-resourceful—Wesker uses Ada, one of the more imaginative characters, to express this central conflict of the play as an image: 'Even a flower can grow in the jungle, can't it? . . . But there's still the jungle, struggling for its own existence, and the sick screeching of animals terrified of each other.' Sarah's philosophy is to combat the jungle, plucking the incidental flower of happiness as compensation during the struggle. But her less tolerant children are too appalled by the jungle to come to grips with it; and less persistent friends like Monty Blatt—the young revolutionary who becomes a well-to-do shop-keeper—accept the jungle for the sole reward of its flowers.

The persistent, unifying movement of the play is towards indifference or bitterness, but at any one point the range of characters illustrates a spectrum of similar but varying attitudes: Monty Blatt's original revolutionary zeal is as superficial as his final materialism, whereas Dave (who becomes Ada's husband) is introspective and serious in both idealism and disillusion. The decline of all these characters is accordingly not uniform but delicately adjusted to the personality of each. Harry's escapist shiftiness becomes an almost willed paralysis: from being the man who takes refuge at his mother's house, he regresses into virtual babyhood again, and his excitable temper dwindles to petulance. Sarah is the central character not only by virtue of her energetic, dominating behaviour but through her lonely insistence on standing by her early hopes, against all evidence and persuasion. Nevertheless she too grows older, her fiery personality is more fitfully active and the last act shows, pathetically, what seems somehow a *smaller* woman, though capable still of terrific effort. Monty defines her as the sort of person who sees everything in black and white: the truth emerges by a strange twist as just the reverse of this. All the *other* characters reject their shared aspirations because *they* see the world and society as too black compared with their own shining hopes: Sarah's last scene reveals the understanding that lies behind her optimism and establishes that, on the contrary, it is she who has taken the really mature attitude of patience and persistence in the face of the greatest discouragement.

The close of the play is characteristically ambiguous and the curtain falls on a confrontation between the defiantly cynical Ronnie and Sarah's cry: 'If you don't care, you'll die.' But the conviction of Sarah's character weighs very strongly here. Initially she had been set against her efficient, trade-union organizing sister-in-law Cissie, whom she calls 'cold': this is incomprehensible to Sarah whose universal benevolence so outfaces her daughter, and she stresses: 'You have to start with love. How can you talk about socialism otherwise?' This basic human warmth is regarded by Sarah not only as the one dependable thing in life—where Monty Blatt stops short—but as the basis of her philosophy and justification of her tenacity: and the title of the play draws attention to this. During the hard times of the twenties, the chicken soup was generously given by a neighbour to Ada, then a very sick child: at the same time Harry temporarily deserted his family. Between the generosity and the desertion, the title indicates where the emphasis lies.

Roots (1959) on the other hand gives, against appearances, a negative not a positive hint in its title. Its characters are farm-working families in Norfolk, and their only connexion with the Kahns and the rest of the trilogy is through Beatie Bryant, the play's central character, who is engaged to Ronnie. But though the Bryants work on the land, the roots in question are not those of the countryman in his traditional way of life. Wesker elsewhere describes the title as showing his 'obsession with beginnings'—but this is misleading, because when Beatie says, 'I come from a family o' farm labourers yet I ent got no roots—just like town people', she is not talking about a sense of history, of the past, but of roots as used for nourishment and holding on: as representing a very present sense of unity with all that a society does and is.

Beatie herself, though initially complacent about her narrow view of the world, spends the first two acts—her holiday first with her married sister Jennie Beales and then with her parents—in trying to work out, according to the half-understood standards picked up from Ronnie, what exactly is lacking in her family's and her own life. This lack she comes to define as rootlessness, the recurrent theme of misunderstanding, compartmentalization, fragmentation. Not having any over-all comprehension of their world, the characters here cannot grasp the connexions between public and personal activity—Mrs Bryant, for instance, regards the existence of popular music as a natural phenomenon rather than dependent on the acquiescence of listeners like herself.

Unlike the earlier plays, *Roots* centres on one dominant character, and Beatie's career through the play embodies the problems of the uncomprehending person in a particularly emphatic way. This is due to the awareness Ronnie has instilled in her that there is actually a problem to solve. He has been trying to give her enough knowledge to acquire some perspective on life, and apparently in London she pretends to understand, in the hope that he will marry her—when she can at once drop the pretence. However, though

Beatie remarks on her prompt reversion to her old self in the country, she tells her sister that she could no longer be satisfied with anything less than the stimulating and demanding life Ronnie has introduced to her.

So Beatie is here in an ambivalent state: she has not attained the capacity to relate and judge information, yet she has rejected the narrowness of the Bryants' way of looking at things. Her uneasy, temporary adjustment consists in quoting Ronnie and trying to explain him to her family. Time and time again this effort breaks down when the puzzled Bryants ask for the rationale behind Ronnie's assumptions. Beatie has the bits and pieces of knowledge—but she still cannot manipulate them, and use them logically to construct her own arguments. Then, suddenly, in the last scene, as the family is assembled to meet Ronnie, a letter arrives to say he is breaking off his engagement to Beatie, because he despairs of her ever achieving or intending sympathy with his beliefs. The pain and humiliation for her are enormous, and somehow the urgent need to understand how she—and by extension the life she was bred to—are not what Ronnie wants, pushes her over the threshold of comprehension. The emotional crisis shocks her mind into a racing intellectual activity, and in the resulting flood of passionate explanation she begins to relate one fact to another, and realizes all at once that she is articulate in her own right at last.

This final, dramatic conversion provides an emphatic and moving climax for the play, of course, though some critics have found such a result of Beatie's jilting improbable, and others consider her new articulacy to be as much a patchwork of Ronnie's ideas as before. A careful examination of the unfolding of Beatie's character does, however, rebut these points: the fact is that her character—like those in *Chicken Soup*—does develop consistently. To begin with, she has always been articulate, in that she chatters irrepressibly to her family and friends: energetic and affectionate, she *wants* to talk to everyone, and there is no sign, in her eagerness to pass on her superficially acquired new notions, of the dumb resentment with which she says she usually greets the outfacing debates of Ronnie's London friends. In this exuberance she is more like the Kahns than the rest of the Bryants. And her sharp-wittedness in seeing isolated failures and inconsistencies in her family's way of life where they specifically affect herself is as clear as her accurate recollection of Ronnie's teachings. Thus, all the elements of a capable, intelligent understanding are already there— very little is needed to remove the barriers of complacency, and in this case it happens to be an emotional shock that provides the motivation: the elements suddenly cohere. And it is a simplification to require that Beatie should prove her articulacy by stating original truths: the more subtle problem the play propounds is that of *relating* knowledge— not discovering it.

One thing to bear in mind is that fragmentation in *Roots*— and Beatie's struggle for articulacy—is not a manifestation of that modern theatrical cliché, the failure of communication. It is *what* to communicate, not *how*, that preoccupies Beatie. But all kinds of communicational failure beset the Bryant family. The female members quarrel among themselves by 'not speaking'—Sister Susan is 'not speaking' so thoroughly that she never appears in the play. And Beatie's sister-in-law Pearl has cut off communications with Mrs Bryant, who in turn, it is said, never speaks to Beatie's grandmother. Sister Jenny's husband and Mr Bryant are simply not given to conversation, and all of them have such a profound sense of privacy that they refuse to discuss, constructively or otherwise, Mr Bryant's loss of job—a reticence that genuinely appals the extrovert Beatie. Apart from the off-stage Ronnie, Stan Mann is almost the only non-Bryant among the characters, and he contrasts with them in his reputation for eccentric behaviour, and on stage in his rambling but speculative language. Independent, enjoying life, he shows some of the individualism that has been worn out of the Bryants, but he is drinking himself to death and, far from offering a hope for the future, is carried off by an ambulance half way through the play.

Though the Bryants are hemmed in and subdued by the proverbially harsh agricultural system, they expand into occasional understated humour that is unlike the exhibition-ist joking of the Kahns, but is nevertheless keen and dry—Beatie's pretensions come in for some deflation here. And the rhythm of the family's Norfolk speech is amazingly different from the rapid flowing cadences of the Kahns and their friends—the changed rhythm showing a more com-prehensive grasp of tone than the superficial local colour of a dialect word of exclamation. And among the characters there is further differentiation, between Stan Mann's slow, backtracking speech, ruminatively savouring his thoughts as they arise, or Jennie's more staccato backtracking for emphasis—as here, recalling childhood rivalry with Beatie's 'Many's the time I'd've willingly strangled you—with no prayers—there you are, no prayers whatsoever. Strangled you till you was dead', or Mrs Bryant's more mechanical repetitions 'Well if he don't reckon we count nor nothin', then it's as well he didn't come. There! It's as well he didn't come.'

The Bryants' taciturnity affects the whole development of the play: a lot of the action is unaccompanied by dialogue, as during an apparently normal but total silence among the assembled Bryants. Wesker's stage direction comments, 'It is not an awkward silence, just a conversationless room', and he warns during Act I: 'The silences are important—as important as the way they speak if we are to know them'. He can allow this silence because the subdued tenor of this kind of life is an essential element in *Roots*. It is the force of environment again that imprisons the Bryants. Thus the first two leisurely acts build up a panoramic picture of what it means to live in such conditions, and this panorama is far more important than the eventual spectacular reversals of Beatie's jilting and her sudden articulacy. As Beatie tests the possibility of escaping from this environment, its strength must be presented and felt—the strength of nineteen years' conditioning that is pitted against Ronnie's three years' influence.

I'm Talking About Jerusalem (1960) combines elements from the first two parts of the trilogy in that it shows two members of the politically-conscious Kahn family living in the Norfolk countryside. Ada and her husband Dave Simmonds are first seen moving into a cottage even more primitive than Jenny Beales', where Dave intends to set up as a craftsman carpenter. Everyone opposes this retreat from urban civilization, and in the last scene the couple move out again, back to London to try something else. Their idea had been to live the kind of life that their friends were only projecting as a future goal for society in general—the integration of work and home, man and environment. After the long scene-painting acts of *Roots*, Wesker here returns to the shorter episodes of *Chicken Soup*—and this perhaps suggests an unsatisfactory aspect of the play, since one of its subjects is the possibility of 'living in mystic bloody communion with nature, indeed' as Beatie would put it. But does this compensating union with the countryside ever take place? The episodic scenes present only the series of frustrating setbacks that finally defeat the Simmonds, and of their passages of more peaceful and continuous life there is little trace.

Again the title is an ironic, negative one: Jerusalem is never built and Dave and Ada are grimly disinclined to embody their vision in words—much to the communicative Sarah's irritation: 'A cold English, you-go-your-way-and-I'll-go-mine' she calls it, and Ada counters: 'Because language is no use. Because we talk about one thing and you hear another, that's why.' And later Dave explodes: 'You bloody Kahns you! You all talk. Sarah, Ronnie, the lot of you. I talked enough! I wanted to *do* something.' So the 'talking' of the title is translated symbolically into actions.

This unwillingness to talk is consonant with the Simmonds' attitude towards their experiment and the rest of the world: they are isolated in more than a topographical sense, in that they are building their individual Jerusalem in defiance of a society they despair of convincing or changing. The difficulties of this solitary exercise lie in the actual impossibility of self-sufficiency: the criticism or hostility of their friends and relations undermine their morale; the uncooperative behaviour of customers, an apprentice, even a van-driver exert pressure on Dave's non-industrialized production-line. Sarah stresses this in the moving-out scene: 'I'm always telling you you can't change the world on your own.'

And perhaps the Simmonds' defiance attracts the rebuffs that are dealt them. In one scene Dave accuses the aunts Esther and Cissie of meanness of attitude—no one has encouraged him. Yet they answer that they have not after all been invited to support the experiment. Each scene sets up a situation in which characters representing some facet of the general hostility appear: the aunts argue for the maintenance of the family unit; Sammy the apprentice sets higher factory wages against freedom and the satisfaction of craftsmanship, and leaves Dave; an admired wartime friend, Libby Dobson, reappears as an embittered, usually drunk, ageing man, who has himself tried this contradiction in terms, a non-capitalistic business, and failed.

In fact Dave and Ada weather most of these tribulations, in the course of which their quality of determination if not sheer stubbornness wears its way through the original appearance of hopeful confidence. Dave's more optimistic, more easily downcast personality proves quite as firm as Ada's rock-like assurance. Structurally the play is centred on their line of action as a couple, and their occasional dissensions are less important than their common attitude.

The mood of the last act is one of only occasionally relieved depression, not least on the part of Ronnie, who has been using the Simmonds' venture as a test-case for the viability of an ideally socialized way of life. It is easy to see this—as practically all Wesker's plays except *Roots* and *The*

Friends can be seen—as a prophecy of hopelessness, of the failure of any ameliorative efforts: but I have tried to indicate the qualifications that result in the effect of the whole play being different from that of its last few lines. The Simmonds' Jerusalem exists in a rather selfish heresy: the 'building alone' that Sarah declares, and experience proves, to be impossible. The solution 'on a personal level' cannot succeed without the co-operation of outsiders or some bending of standards. Libby Dobson rightly pointed out that almost every object in their frugal lives had still been produced by an underpaid, unfulfilled worker at a monotonous assembly line—they cannot disclaim complicity in the unfairness of society at the same time as they benefit from it. Nonetheless they do refuse to be defeated: Dave still has the energy, physical and spiritual, to go on, and this demonstration of revival after defeat inspires a sort of resilience even in the mercurial Ronnie. *Chicken Soup* ended with the warning that one must care; and *Jerusalem* adds that one must also learn *not* to care for opposition and defeat.

IV

The short scenes of *Chicken Soup* and *Jerusalem* had their birth primarily in Wesker's naturalistic attitude to lengthy narratives—he was unwilling to distort the detailed living pictures he needed to present in order to achieve unity of time and place. But the shortness of certain scenes did serve also to frame and underline the importance of each, and, if anything, Act III, scene ii of *Chicken Soup* and Act II, scene i of *Jerusalem* which both fall naturally into two parts, could well have gained by further formal division. In *Chips with Everything* (1962) Wesker begins to make a positive virtue of the episodic short-scene structure, on which the scenes of *Chips* are systematically based. The effect of this technique is that the logical step-by-step development of the plot is emphasized. Each stage has its autonomous im-

portance, pointed by the dramatic full-stop of its scene-
ending, and the crowding, changing situations give the
action a sense of speed.

Again the plot deals with a failure—the failure of Pip,
a rich man's son doing his National Service, to help his
fellow-conscripts in opposing the unfair, often ridiculous
and repressive Air Force system. As a well-educated upper-
class conscript, he is singled out from his working-class
companions by his superiors for officer training. He refuses
—and he also refuses to perform the barbarous bayonet
drill. The crisis occurs when Smiler, the scapegoat of the
hut where Pip and eight others live, runs away from the
intolerable persecution and returns, hopeless and vulnerable,
to the camp he knows he cannot really escape. All unite to
present an increasingly dangerous front of defiance to the
officer who comes to arrest Smiler—all, that is, except Pip
who suavely smoothes over the situation and avoids the
confrontation so that everything returns to normal. He,
meanwhile, quietly joins the officers as a trainee.

Pip is a complex character, and indeed he does not know
his own motives at first, which partly explains his crucial
volte-face. The clue lies once more in the distinction between rebellion and revolution that the plays often pose:
Pip is, in the last analysis, purely destructive in impulse, and,
crudely, he is only extending his rebellion against his father
who was a general, against the officers and the system that
are associated with his father. The intimate, probing
interrogations of the strange, soft-spoken Pilot Officer
reveal however that Pip subconsciously desires power too—
in classically Oedipal fashion—to replace his domineering
father: he does not in short have the qualities to build
constructively, only to destroy, and the alternative ideal of
equality and brotherhood, which his friends demonstrate in
their united defence of Smiler, is quite alien to his complicated but self-assertive nature.

An early scene during which Pip shows his tendency to
dominate becomes one of the highlights of the play in

performance. He devises and organizes a complicated manœuvre to steal a bag of coke for his hut one cold winter's night: this involves an elaborate rushing to and fro with bags and stools to climb over a wire fence, each phase breathlessly executed between the regular patrolling of the sentry. The silence, the tension and the speed punctuated by the unobservant sentry's pacing make a very funny pattern of stage business, and this brisk yet balletic piece of mime belongs rather with the frantic, almost farcical 'service' in *The Kitchen* than with the leisurely naturalistic activity of the trilogy. Early in his relationship with his hutmates Pip had recounted a parable of the French Revolution, when the unexpectedly assembled commoners 'looked at themselves and realized that there were more of them than they ever imagined': both there and in his later indignation at being praised for his 'leadership' of the coke-stealing episode (he rejects the necessity of 'leaders'), Pip is arguing against the grain of his assertive personality. The masterminded coke-stealing forms the tenth scene of the first part of *Chips*: and, at the same point of the second part, is another 'set piece' scene—the long monologue delivered by Smiler, running on the spot, which abstracts and represents the whole of his hopeless circular escape through rage, bewilderment and despair. The monologue is naturalistic in that it is typical of Smiler, but stylized in its telescoping of a much longer process: and its significance as well as its form balances its counterpart in Act II, for whereas the whole hut crowded round to praise Pip after the coke-stealing, Smiler's flight brings the whole hut to care for and defend him unanimously—without a leader.

As the extraordinary, machine-like coke-stealing performance and Smiler's stylized escape suggest, Wesker was here moving away from the naturalism of the trilogy, and in the officer characters he proceeded to a deliberate caricature that is all the more emphatic for their first appearance being at the initiatory lecture, set up on the platform like music-hall turns. Again, Wesker's ear for dialogue differentiates between the officers' speeches as they lecture, and later he turns Corporal Hill's hypnotic flow of information and orders into another set piece, the opportunity for an actor's *tour de force*. Sometimes the speech levels are ambiguous—is the Pilot Officer's intoned warning 'we listen but we do not hear, we befriend but we do not touch you, we applaud but we do not act' an instance of stylization, or realistic evidence of a psychotic character? But unquestionably successful is Pip's first long speech, his putting down of conversational skirmishing during which he is accused of snobbery. Obliquely he replies with the story of his visit to an East End café and the resulting sense of being in an utterly alien world. This would function in a novel as interior monologue, and in an older dramatic tradition as soliloquy—it has the tone of reverie. Pip's delicately repeated refrain is 'strange—I don't know why I should have been so surprised' (the gap between theory and real feeling is being foreshadowed). The speech has the haunting prose rhythm that was to illuminate long sections of *The Four Seasons*, and which had already appeared in Beatie's reverie-like speech recalling her relationship with Ronnie in *Roots*.

The exuberance of *Chips* is supported by the usually irrepressible spirits of the sorely tried but very young conscripts. Wesker's next play, *Their Very Own and Golden City* (1966) deals with an essentially similar topic, the absorption of a rebel into society. However, here the process takes not the eight weeks of *Chips*, but the seventy odd years from 1926 to 1990, and thus the gradual discouragement of its ageing characters weighs heavily at least on the latter part of the play. *Chips*, with its microcosmic, closed Air Force world, reflected society in almost as diminished a form as had *The Kitchen*, and *Golden City*, while extending more deeply and directly into society *per se*, also takes one specific enterprise, the building of a truly innovatory 'new town', as an allegory for any kind of profound social change.

The tragic element in *Golden City* lies in the likeable, even potentially great central character Andrew Cobham whose failure, unlike Pip's, is painfully unintentional. As a young architect, Andy and his friends Paul and Stoney, and his future wife Jessie, plan a set of six 'Golden Cities' that will be owned entirely by their inhabitants who will have the freedom to fulfil themselves and to experiment with the organization of work and leisure, free from external pressures. In middle age the friends set about realizing this project, but unfortunately they themselves are not yet protected from external pressures, and gradually the six cities dwindle to one, the ownership of its factories and plants passes into the hands of outside financiers, and when at last the city is built it is just like any other city—except for the quality of its architecture, which ironically earns Andy a knighthood. The city—as Dave Simmonds had already discovered—obviously has the vulnerability of being one isolated unit in a hostile world: what is different about this Jerusalem is that its builders start out fully conscious of the danger, and resolve to continue even against all hope to 'ignore history', with an obstinacy that has a certain nobility. The situation, and consequently the whole play, is thus more sophisticated than that of the earlier *Jerusalem*.

Because the friends begin from the premise that in building a city they will 'build the habits of a way of life in that city', the environment issue is necessarily explicit, but its effect—the effect of circumstances—on Andy is more subtle. Does he ruin the city or does the city ruin him? Certainly the cynical, callous old man of the last scene is as different from the ardent clowning young visionary as the eventual 'model town' is from the originally projected chain of blessed communities. At various stages Andy's growing hardness allows him to betray both the vision and his fellow-workers, besides the would-be city-dwellers, for the sake of immediate progress. Conversely the anxiety and discouragement of the task sours his marriage and his temper, and ultimately destroys his self-respect. Yet always the obstacles are so formidable that the only progress possible seems to lie through some small betrayal. This is Wesker's most comprehensive expression of the fusion of personality and circumstance in motivating action: on public and private fronts, in Andy's political manœuvres and architectural integrity, in his relations with his wife Jessie, and with Kate, who loves him, the interaction of every influence and incident with the next is unobtrusive but inexorable.

But this interrelationship does not imply impenetrable confusion: somewhere the seeds of failure can be detected, and in spite of the strong environmental theme it seems that Andy is responsible for the initial error. The friend and mentor of Andy's early years is Jake Latham, a cannily-drawn, wise old trade-unionist politician, but for the sake of local party unity Andy's first public speech has to be a refutation of Jake's divisive policies. And the point is that Andy fails not by opposing his old friend, but by going too far, by using unfair, emotional rhetoric: in fact he progressively loses his 'high seriousness' by treating some incidents as unworthy of his full involvement—as side issues, where he need not bother to act thoughtfully or sympathetically. This is the crux: Andy cannot keep his sense of integrity, and of course one callous act makes the next, bigger betrayal easier, and so on. Jake's role is significant, for he is the character who formulates the basic conflict between immobilized idealism and self-destructive compromise—it is the example that counts, he concludes, and the untold effect of good or bad actions for good or bad on future generations.

Wesker poignantly stresses the cumulative effect of Andy's compromises by punctuating the series of short *Chips*-like scenes with flashbacks to the opening situation—a visit by the young friends to Durham Cathedral. Their enthusiasm and their visions of the future counterpoint more and more ironically those narrative scenes that cover the years to 1948: and after this Wesker uses a 'flash forward'

scene which projects into the future what might or 'does'
happen, without formal divisions and in a more continuous
dream-like flow. There are no more flashbacks until the
very end, when a card party between Kate, the defeated,
aged Andy and a minister and a business man—two of the
characters who have defeated him—gives way to a scene in
which the young Andy, Jessie, Stoney and Paul, apparently
shut in the Cathedral, finally find the last door that is open.
A sign of hope? Anyway a sad, ironical hope, set as it is
against the grim card party, but typical of Wesker's poetic
use of stage symbol. The Golden City itself—which never
appears on stage—is obviously less of a concrete fact than a
poetic image, even when built, and the Cathedral is another
appropriately architectural symbol of men's visions—yet it
too, as the last scene warns, can imprison the spirit that
informs it.

V

In that Andrew Cobham lost his integrity initially by
differentiating between important issues, where he con-
sidered that he must behave scrupulously, and unimportant
issues, where he could be brutal, *Golden City* comprehends
Wesker's fragmentation theme with the more obvious
concern with environment. Concurrently with *Golden City*,
however, Wesker wrote *The Four Seasons* (1965) which
develops a new preoccupation. 'Even when Jerusalem is
built', says Adam, one of its two characters, 'friends will
grow apart and mothers will mourn their sons growing old.'
This concern is with private pain, and appropriately the two
characters Adam and Beatrice are each locked in a solitary
world of private needs, griefs and resentments. Adam has
betrayed his wife and been betrayed by his mistress, and
Beatrice is similarly bruised from a bitter relationship with
husband and lover: but both try once more, unsuccessfully,
to realize a new chance of happiness with each other.

This is Wesker's most pessimistic play to date, eclipsing the ambiguous, provisional defeats of the trilogy, *Chips* and *Golden City*. For Adam and Beatrice find themselves damned by their past as effectively as any Greek offenders against the gods, simply because the habit of betrayal and suspicion is ineradicable, and poisons the most determinedly fresh start. Formally the closest comparison is with *The Kitchen*, for, as the title suggests, *The Four Seasons* has a cyclical framework, being divided into four equal parts—Winter, Spring, Summer and Autumn—while the burden of the play is the inevitability of recurrence. Where *The Kitchen* had suggested ways of breaking out of the cycle, *The Four Seasons* allows no reservations, checks or balances: its key words are 'always' and 'never'.

It is probably the absolute quality, the universality that is so thinly veiled, that weakens this play—the anonymous faded set (an abandoned though furnished house), the isolation of the two characters, their detachment from everyday society. The web of personal living that is needed to clothe such archetypal figures is not spun out of the characters' language—everything is relentlessly significant without at the same time existing solidly in its own right. This is not to deny the poetry of Wesker's prose, particularly in Adam's and Beatrice's reminiscences, but the characters themselves fail to rise to the level of their speeches.

Arguably the text of *The Four Seasons* might be illuminated by a more inspired production than has yet been staged: Wesker's next play however, *The Friends* (1970), is a powerfully impressive achievement in spite of a generally underrated première directed by its author. The theme of private pain is here developed more characteristically and successfully through the personal but parallel anguish of a group of friends, one of whose number, the dominant and much-loved Esther, dies half way through the play, releasing in each profound fears of death and ageing. *The Friends* appeared in the same year as the volume of essays, *Fears of Fragmentation*, and could well have borne the same title, for

the friends' private pain is their reaction to the hetero-
geneous muddle their experience now seems to them.
Roland, Esther's lover, springs from cult to cult, trying to
find salvation in a ready-made system; Crispin's defensive
bitchiness covers an inexplicable penchant for love affairs
with old women; Tessa's comic cultivation of anger has
hardened into a reflex that threatens her with unaccepted
age; Simone's need to be needed frightens her into an un-
appealing timidity; and, symptomatic of all these facets of
incompetence in living, Manfred, Esther's brother, explicitly recognizes his basic incapacity to weigh, balance and
evaluate theories and sensations.

Thus all the friends—and also Macey, the angst-ridden
older manager of their shops—are in the vertiginous
position of being bombarded by fragments of experience
which strike them as equally valuable or worthless, they
do not know which. Necessarily, then, not being able to
cope with life, they certainly cannot cope with death, and
as they see Esther dying and are confronted with a mirror-
image of their own death, each one is panic-stricken by the
conviction that his own life and its end will be meaningless.

Different strands of Wesker's technique are drawn
together here. The theme is reflected in the situation, as
in *Golden City*—and in the set, as in *Roots*. The shops—we
hear, significantly, of their impending bankruptcy in the
first scene—where the group exploit their exclusively
twentieth-century interior designs, are as cut off from a
sense of tradition or unity with the past and future as the
friends themselves are psychologically cut off from all the
chaotic experience they do not know how to use. And the
room in which all the action takes place embodies the
potential richness of this experience—its tapestries, books,
collages, models, new designs, antiques.

Here Wesker is reverting to the first and essential task of
deciding upon one's values. For Esther, whose room this is,
loves life, and this is because she alone has worked out
standards of right and wrong, beautiful and ugly, useful and

pernicious, that equip her to measure and reject or accept her experiences. To some extent her knowledge is shared theoretically by Macey the outsider and Simone the scape-goat, whose unhappiness is at least partly imposed by others, and they urge the group to accept Esther's solution, the solution which had enabled her to avoid their crippling defeatism. And as in *Roots*, the intellectual conversion is stimulated by an emotional charge: having created his values in Esther and killed them with her, Wesker as it were resurrects them in the last scene when, in a weird and mov-ing ritual, Simone lifts up the dead woman, and symbolically brings her back into the circle of friends, who accept in her both death and the living past.

Once more the shape of the play adapts to its full meaning. The action is limited within the twenty-four hours of the neo-classical unity of time, but significantly this does *not* contribute to a sense of such closed, cyclical unity as *The Kitchen*: the play opens in the early evening, and later Esther dies. The following scenes during the night show the group suffering the darkness of despair—especially Roland who is rendered literally dumb by panic and misery. Then in the morning Macey and Simone force their friends to attack their problems again, and it is at the start of a new, unpredictable, different day that the curtain falls, leaving a sense not of recurrence but of a new beginning.

Unlike many of his erratic contemporaries, Wesker has steadily improved his mastery of theme and technique, as the brightness of the early plays gives way to a more subtle shading of richer colours. Naturally, only a provisional assessment of Wesker's work can be made at this stage of his writing career: however, the very steadiness of his development so far suggests that he will not waste energy on uncharacteristic dead-end experiments, but will evolve with-in his own line of continuity. He has always had an ear for dialogue and an assured sense of form; this has been re-inforced by a new dramatic poetry while the more awkward moments of exposition and occasional didacticism of the trilogy have been eliminated. The label of simple social dramatist that was initially hung like a millstone round Wesker's neck has necessarily hindered assessment of his far-from-simple plays, but as he continues to show (for example) the delicate control of dialogue evident in the Chekhovian opening of *The Friends*, where several strands of conversation are counterpointed musically and ironically, the sheer persuasive quality of his writing must elicit recognition of his stature as a dramatist.

ARNOLD WESKER

A Select Bibliography

(Place of publication London, unless otherwise stated)

Separate Works:

CHICKEN SOUP WITH BARLEY (1959).

ROOTS (1959).

THE KITCHEN (1960)

—first version in *New English Dramatists*, *2*, edited by E. M. Browne; full length version, 1961.

I'M TALKING ABOUT JERUSALEM (1960).

CHIPS WITH EVERYTHING: A Play in two acts (1962).

THE FOUR SEASONS (1966)

—also published in *New English Dramatists*, *9*, 1966.

THEIR VERY OWN AND GOLDEN CITY: A Play in two acts and twenty-nine scenes (1966).

THE FRIENDS: A Play in two acts (1970).

FEARS OF FRAGMENTATION (1970). *Collection of Lectures and Articles*

SIX SUNDAYS IN JANUARY (1971). *Collection of Short Stories and Short Plays*

—contains: 'Pools', a short story; 'The Nottingham Captain', a moral for Narrator, Voices and Orchestra; *Menace*, a play for television; 'Six Sundays in January', a long short story; 'The London Diary for Stockholm.'

Collections:

THE WESKER TRILOGY (1960).

Some Critical Studies

'Arnold Wesker as a Playwright', by C. Spencer, *The Jewish Quarterly*, Winter 1959-60, 40-1.

MID-CENTURY DRAMA, by L. Kitchin (1960)

—second and revised ed., 1962; includes a chapter 'Theatre in the Raw'.

'Plays and Politics', by R. Findlater, *Twentieth Century*, CLXVIII, September 1960, 235-42.

'The Theatre of Arnold Wesker', by A. R. Jones, *Critical Quarterly*, II, 1960, 366-70.

'The New Dramatists, 2: Arnold Wesker', by H. Goodman, *Drama Survey*, I, 1961, 215-22.

'What Though the Field Be Lost?', by N. Dennis, *Encounter*, August 1962, 43-5.

ANGER AND AFTER, by J. Russell Taylor (1962)

—revised edition, 1969; includes a chapter 'Productions Out of Town: Arnold Wesker'.

'Wesker's "Centre 42" ', by J. Lee, *Encounter*, August 1962, 95-6.

'Oh Mother Is It Worth It?', by C. Marowitz, *Theatre Arts*, May 1962, 21-2, 72-3.

EXPERIMENTAL DRAMA, ed. W. A. Armstrong (1963)

—contains a chapter 'Drama with a Message: Arnold Wesker', by L. Kitchin.

'Sartre and Wesker: Committed Playwrights', by M. Andereth, *Comment*, V, July-August 1964, 18-28.

THE THEATRE OF PARADOX AND PROTEST: Developments in the avant-garde drama, by G. E. Wellwarth (1965)

—includes a chapter 'Arnold Wesker: Awake and Sing in White-chapel'.

ARNOLD WESKER, by H. U. Ribalow; New York (1965).

'Roots: a Reassessment', by J. Latham, *Modern Drama*, VIII, 1965, 192-7.

'Arnold Wesker: the Last Humanist', by M. Anderson, *New Theatre Magazine*, VIII, 3, 1968, 10-27.

ARNOLD WESKER, by R. Hayman (1970)

—in the 'Contemporary Playwrights' series.

TIMES AUTHORS SERIES NO. 1: ARNOLD WESKER, ed. M. Marland (1970).

THE PLAYS OF ARNOLD WESKER, by Glenda Leeming and S. Trussler (1971).

WRITERS AND THEIR WORK

General Surveys:

THE DETECTIVE STORY IN BRITAIN:
Julian Symons
THE ENGLISH BIBLE: Donald Coggan
ENGLISH VERSE EPIGRAM:
G. Rostrevor Hamilton
ENGLISH HYMNS: A. Pollard
ENGLISH MARITIME WRITING:
Hakluyt to Cook: Oliver Warner
THE ENGLISH SHORT STORY I: & II:
T. O. Beachcroft
THE ENGLISH SONNET: P. Cruttwell
ENGLISH SERMONS: Arthur Pollard
ENGLISH TRANSLATORS and
TRANSLATIONS: J. M. Cohen
ENGLISH TRAVELLERS IN THE
NEAR EAST: Robin Fedden
THREE WOMEN DIARISTS: M. Willy

Sixteenth Century and Earlier:

FRANCIS BACON: J. Max Patrick
BEAUMONT & FLETCHER: Ian Fletcher
CHAUCER: Nevill Coghill
GOWER & LYDGATE: Derek Pearsall
RICHARD HOOKER: A. Pollard
THOMAS KYD: Philip Edwards
LANGLAND: Nevill Coghill
LYLY & PEELE: G. K. Hunter
MALORY: M. C. Bradbrook
MARLOWE: Philip Henderson
SIR THOMAS MORE: E. E. Reynolds
RALEGH: Agnes Latham
SIDNEY: Kenneth Muir
SKELTON: Peter Green
SPENSER: Rosemary Freeman
THREE 14TH-CENTURY ENGLISH
MYSTICS: Phyllis Hodgson
TWO SCOTS CHAUCERIANS:
H. Harvey Wood
WYATT: Sergio Baldi

Seventeenth Century:

SIR THOMAS BROWNE: Peter Green
BUNYAN: Henri Talon
CAVALIER POETS: Robin Skelton
CONGREVE: Bonamy Dobrée
DONNE: F. Kermode
DRYDEN: Bonamy Dobrée
ENGLISH DIARISTS:
Evelyn and Pepys: M. Willy
FARQUHAR: A. J. Farmer
JOHN FORD: Clifford Leech
GEORGE HERBERT: T. S. Eliot
HERRICK: John Press
HOBBES: T. E. Jessop
BEN JONSON: J. B. Bamborough
LOCKE: Maurice Cranston

ANDREW MARVELL: John Press
MILTON: E. M. W. Tillyard
RESTORATION COURT POETS:
V. de S. Pinto
SHAKESPEARE: C. J. Sisson
CHRONICLES: Clifford Leech
EARLY COMEDIES: Derek Traversi
LATER COMEDIES: G. K. Hunter
FINAL PLAYS: F. Kermode
HISTORIES: L. C. Knights
POEMS: F. T. Prince
PROBLEM PLAYS: Peter Ure
ROMAN PLAYS: T. J. B. Spencer
GREAT TRAGEDIES: Kenneth Muir
THREE METAPHYSICAL POETS:
Margaret Willy
WEBSTER: Ian Scott-Kilvert
WYCHERLEY: P. F. Vernon

Eighteenth Century:

BERKELEY: T. E. Jessop
BLAKE: Kathleen Raine
BOSWELL: P. A. W. Collins
BURKE: T. E. Utley
BURNS: David Daiches
WM. COLLINS: Oswald Doughty
COWPER: N. Nicholson
CRABBE: R. L. Brett
DEFOE: J. R. Sutherland
FIELDING: John Butt
GAY: Oliver Warner
GIBBON: C. V. Wedgwood
GOLDSMITH: A. Norman Jeffares
GRAY: R. W. Ketton-Cremer
HUME: Montgomery Belgion
SAMUEL JOHNSON: S. C. Roberts
POPE: Ian Jack
RICHARDSON: R. F. Brissenden
SHERIDAN: W. A. Darlington
CHRISTOPHER SMART: G. Grigson
SMOLLETT: Laurence Brander
STEELE, ADDISON: A. R. Humphreys
STERNE: D. W. Jefferson
SWIFT: J. Middleton Murry
SIR JOHN VANBRUGH: Bernard Harris
HORACE WALPOLE: Hugh Honour

Nineteenth Century:

MATTHEW ARNOLD: Kenneth Allott
JANE AUSTEN: S. Townsend Warner
BAGEHOT: N. St John-Stevas
BRONTË SISTERS: Phyllis Bentley
BROWNING: John Bryson
E. B. BROWNING: Alethea Hayter
SAMUEL BUTLER: G. D. H. Cole
BYRON: I, II & III Bernard Blackstone
CARLYLE: David Gascoyne

LEWIS CARROLL: Derek Hudson
COLERIDGE: Kathleen Raine
CREEVEY & GREVILLE: J. Richardson
DE QUINCEY: Hugh Sykes Davies
DICKENS: K. J. Fielding
  EARLY NOVELS: T. Blount
  LATER NOVELS: B. Hardy
DISRAELI: Paul Bloomfield
GEORGE ELIOT: Lettice Cooper
FERRIER & GALT: W. M. Parker
FITZGERALD: Joanna Richardson
ELIZABETH GASKELL: Miriam Allott
GISSING: A. C. Ward
THOMAS HARDY: R. A. Scott-James
              and C. Day Lewis
HAZLITT: J. B. Priestley
HOOD: Laurence Brander
G. M. HOPKINS: Geoffrey Grigson
T. H. HUXLEY: William Irvine
KEATS: Edmund Blunden
LAMB: Edmund Blunden
LANDOR: G. Rostrevor Hamilton
EDWARD LEAR: Joanna Richardson
MACAULAY: G. R. Potter
MEREDITH: Phyllis Bartlett
JOHN STUART MILL: M. Cranston
WILLIAM MORRIS: P. Henderson
NEWMAN: J. M. Cameron
PATER: Ian Fletcher
PEACOCK: J. I. M. Stewart
ROSSETTI: Oswald Doughty
CHRISTINA ROSSETTI: G. Battiscombe
RUSKIN: Peter Quennell
SIR WALTER SCOTT: Ian Jack
SHELLEY: G. M. Matthews
SOUTHEY: Geoffrey Carnall
LESLIE STEPHEN: Phyllis Grosskurth
R. L. STEVENSON: G. B. Stern
SWINBURNE: H. J. C. Grierson
TENNYSON: B. C. Southam
THACKERAY: Laurence Brander
FRANCIS THOMPSON: P. Butter
TROLLOPE: Hugh Sykes Davies
OSCAR WILDE: James Laver
WORDSWORTH: Helen Darbishire

Twentieth Century:
CHINUA ACHEBE: A. Ravenscroft
W. H. AUDEN: Richard Hoggart
HILAIRE BELLOC: Renée Haynes
ARNOLD BENNETT: F. Swinnerton
EDMUND BLUNDEN: Alec M. Hardie
ROBERT BRIDGES: J. Sparrow
ANTHONY BURGESS: Carol M. Dix
ROY CAMPBELL: David Wright
JOYCE CARY: Walter Allen
G. K. CHESTERTON: C. Hollis
WINSTON CHURCHILL: John Connell

R. G. COLLINGWOOD: E. W. F. Tomlin
I. COMPTON-BURNETT:
              R. Glynn Grylls
JOSEPH CONRAD: Oliver Warner
WALTER DE LA MARE: K. Hopkins
NORMAN DOUGLAS: Ian Greenlees
LAWRENCE DURRELL: G. S. Fraser
T. S. ELIOT: M. C. Bradbrook
FIRBANK & BETJEMAN: J. Brooke
FORD MADOX FORD: Kenneth Young
E. M. FORSTER: Rex Warner
CHRISTOPHER FRY: Derek Stanford
JOHN GALSWORTHY: R. H. Mottram
WM. GOLDING: Clive Pemberton
ROBERT GRAVES: M. Seymour-Smith
GRAHAM GREENE: Francis Wyndham
L. P. HARTLEY: Paul Bloomfield
A. E. HOUSMAN: Ian Scott-Kilvert
ALDOUS HUXLEY: Jocelyn Brooke
HENRY JAMES: Michael Swan
PAMELA H. JOHNSON: Isabel Quigly
JAMES JOYCE: J. I. M. Stewart
RUDYARD KIPLING: Bonamy Dobrée
D. H. LAWRENCE: Kenneth Young
C. DAY LEWIS: Clifford Dyment
WYNDHAM LEWIS: E. W. F. Tomlin
COMPTON MACKENZIE: K. Young
LOUIS MACNEICE: John Press
KATHERINE MANSFIELD: Ian Gordon
JOHN MASEFIELD: L. A. G. Strong
SOMERSET MAUGHAM: J. Brophy
GEORGE MOORE: A. Norman Jeffares
J. MIDDLETON MURRY: Philip Mairet
R. K. NARAYAN: William Walsh
SEAN O'CASEY: W. A. Armstrong
GEORGE ORWELL: Tom Hopkinson
JOHN OSBORNE: Simon Trussler
HAROLD PINTER: John Russell Taylor
POETS OF 1939–45 WAR: R. N. Currey
ANTHONY POWELL: Bernard Bergonzi
POWYS BROTHERS: R. C. Churchill
J. B. PRIESTLEY: Ivor Brown
HERBERT READ: Francis Berry
FOUR REALIST NOVELISTS: V. Brome
BERNARD SHAW: A. C. Ward
EDITH SITWELL: John Lehmann
KENNETH SLESSOR: C. Semmler
C. P. SNOW: William Cooper
SYNGE & LADY GREGORY: E. Coxhead
DYLAN THOMAS: G. S. Fraser
G. M. TREVELYAN: J. H. Plumb
WAR POETS: 1914–18: E. Blunden
EVELYN WAUGH: Christopher Hollis
H. G. WELLS: Montgomery Belgion
PATRICK WHITE: R. F. Brissenden
ANGUS WILSON: K. W. Gransden
VIRGINIA WOOLF: B. Blackstone
W. B. YEATS: G. S. Fraser